BIOGRAPHIES

BENJAMIN FRANKLIN
WRITER, INVENTOR, STATESMAN

Written by Pamela Hill Nettleton
Illustrated by Jeff Yesh

Special thanks to our advisers for their expertise:

Gregory L. Kaster, Ph.D., Chair, Department of History
Gustavus Adolphus College, St. Peter, Minnesota

Susan Kesselring, M.A., Literacy Educator
Rosemount–Apple Valley–Eagan (Minnesota) School District

PICTURE WINDOW BOOKS
MINNEAPOLIS, MINNESOTA

Managing Editor: Bob Temple
Creative Director: Terri Foley
Editor: Peggy Henrikson
Editorial Adviser: Andrea Cascardi
Copy Editor: Laurie Kahn
Page production: The Design Lab
The illustrations in this book were rendered digitally.

PICTURE WINDOW BOOKS

5115 Excelsior Boulevard
Suite 232
Minneapolis, MN 55416
1-877-845-8392
www.picturewindowbooks.com

Printed in the United States of America.

Library of Congress Cataloging-in-Publication Data
Nettleton, Pamela Hill.
Benjamin Franklin : writer, inventor, statesman / written by Pamela Hill
Nettleton ; illustrated by Jeff Yesh.
p. cm. — (Biographies)
Summary: A brief biography that highlights some of the achievements
of one of the most famous men from the early years of the United States.
Includes bibliographical references (p.) and index.
ISBN 1-4048-0186-3
1. Franklin, Benjamin, 1706–1790–Juvenile literature. 2. Statesmen–
United States–Biography–Juvenile literature. 3. Scientists–United
States–Biography–Juvenile literature. 4. Inventors–United States–
Biography–Juvenile literature. 5. Printers–United States–Biography–
Juvenile literature. [1. Franklin, Benjamin, 1706–1790. 2. Statesmen.
3. Scientists. 4. Inventors. 5. Printers.] I. Yesh, Jeff, 1971– ill. II. Title.
E302.6.F8 N48 2003
973.3'092–DC21   2003004124

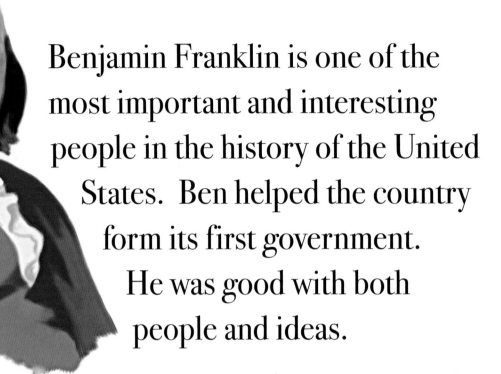

Benjamin Franklin is one of the most important and interesting people in the history of the United States. Ben helped the country form its first government. He was good with both people and ideas.

Ben was very smart and curious, too.
He taught himself how to do many things well.
His inventions and ideas still help us today.

This is the story of Benjamin Franklin.

Benjamin Franklin came from a big family. He had 16 brothers and sisters! He was born in Boston, Massachusetts, in 1706. Massachusetts was then a colony belonging to England.

4

Ben's father had a shop where he made soap and candles. When Ben turned 10, he had to stay home from school and help his father.

Ben learned how to make soap and candles, but he never liked doing it.

Ben got to go to school for only two years, but he read every book he found. He taught himself math, writing, and science.

6

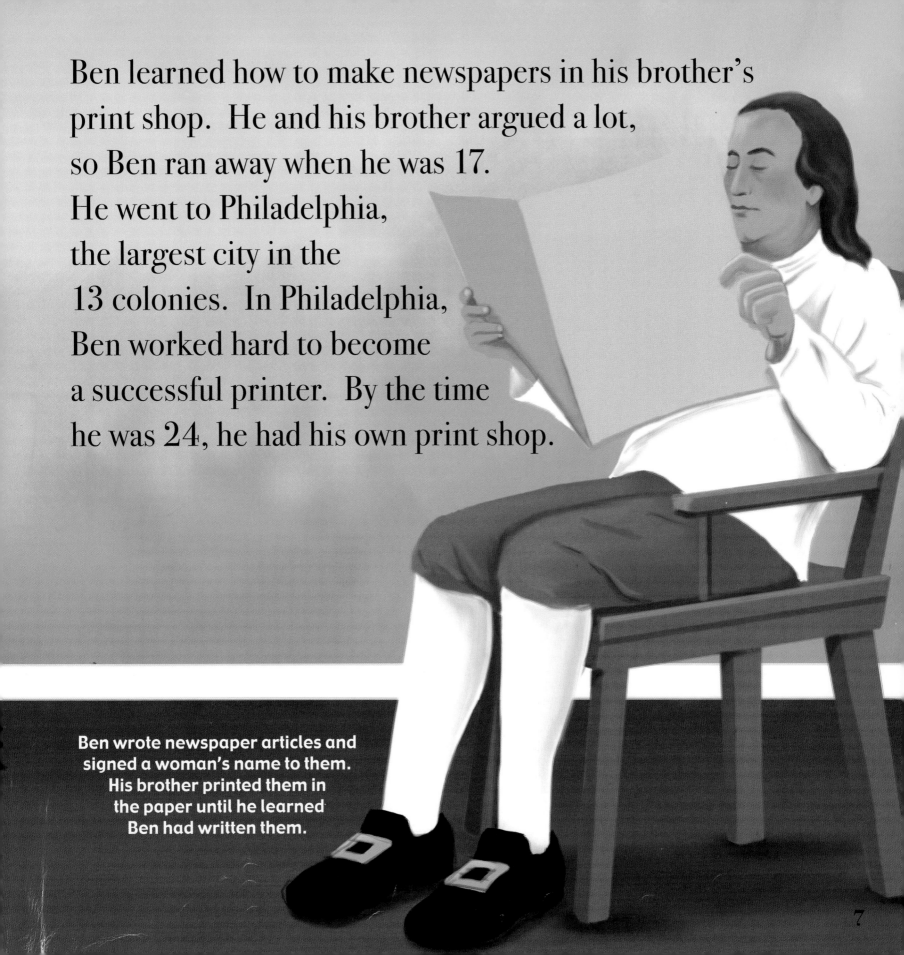

Ben learned how to make newspapers in his brother's print shop. He and his brother argued a lot, so Ben ran away when he was 17. He went to Philadelphia, the largest city in the 13 colonies. In Philadelphia, Ben worked hard to become a successful printer. By the time he was 24, he had his own print shop.

Ben wrote newspaper articles and signed a woman's name to them. His brother printed them in the paper until he learned Ben had written them.

7

Printing Shop

He printed the *Pennsylvania Gazette* newspaper. He also printed a book he wrote called *Poor Richard's Almanac.*

People loved to read Ben's almanac. It was funny and full of wise sayings we still use today.

Some of Ben's sayings:
- "Early to bed and early to rise makes a man healthy, wealthy, and wise."
- "God helps them that help themselves."
- "Little strokes fell great oaks."
- "An ounce of prevention is worth a pound of cure."

In 1730, Ben married Deborah Read. She helped run a general store in front of the print shop. She sold things such as soap and fabrics.

Ben was a happy, funny man.
He was also curious. He had a lot
of questions about the world:
What makes wind blow?
Where does electricity come from?
Why is the ocean warm near the shore?

When Ben had a question, he tried to find the answer.
He wondered if lightning made electricity.

He flew a kite in a storm until lightning hit the kite.
The lightning traveled down the string and hit a key
tied at the other end. It made a spark—electricity!

Ben's experiments with electricity were often dangerous.
He once tried to kill a turkey with electric shock.
Instead, he knocked himself out.

When Ben found
an answer, he used
it to help people.
He invented the
lightning rod,
a tall pole to put
on top of a house.
It kept lightning
from starting fires
in people's
homes.

14

Back then, people heated their homes with wood-burning stoves. Ben invented a stove that burned less wood yet was even hotter than other stoves. It was called the Franklin stove.

Ben never sold anything he invented. He just gave away his ideas to make people's lives better.

Ben ran the post office and helped the mail get delivered faster. In 1775, he became the first postmaster general, in charge of all the post offices in the colonies. In 1847, Ben and George Washington had their pictures on the very first U.S. postage stamps.

Ben helped start the first library, the first fire department, and the first city hospital in the colonies.

Ben's hospital was built especially for the poor. Before this hospital, people who were poor and sick had no place to go for help.

In 1775, the colonies started the Revolutionary War to win their freedom from England. Ben helped write the Declaration of Independence. This important paper marked the beginning of the United States of America.

In CONGRESS July 4 1776.

The unanimous Declaration of the thirteen united States of America.

At first, the war was not going well. Ben went to France. He convinced the French to send their army to help the colonies. Many people think the war would have been lost without Ben's work.

The French people really liked Ben. They painted pictures of him and wrote poems about him. Crowds followed him when he walked down the street.

Ben was honored by putting his face on the $100 bill.

After the war, Ben helped make America's first laws. He signed the Constitution of the United States. The country loved him! He died in 1790, at the age of 84. About 20,000 people went to his funeral.

Ben once said he would like to return to the world 100 years after he died to see all the new ideas and inventions. Imagine what he would say if he visited us today!

THE LIFE OF BENJAMIN FRANKLIN

1706 Born in Boston, Massachusetts, on January 17

1718 Worked with his brother James in a print shop in Boston

1723 Ran away to Philadelphia, Pennsylvania, at age 17

1728 Opened his own print shop, publishing a newspaper and *Poor Richard's Almanac*

1730 Married Deborah Read

1731 Helped start the first library that loaned out books

1736 Founded the Union Fire Company in Philadelphia

1752 Conducted his famous kite experiment

1776 Signed the Declaration of Independence

1778 Signed the Treaty of Alliance with France to get France's help for the colonies

1783 Signed the Treaty of Paris, ending the Revolutionary War

1787 Signed the Constitution of the United States

1790 Died in Philadelphia on April 17, at age 84

DID YOU KNOW?

⚘ Ben got tired of taking his glasses on and off to read, so he invented bifocals. These special glasses help people see both near and far.

⚘ Ben sailed back and forth between America and France many times. He used his time on the ship to study ocean currents and temperatures.

⚘ Ben was one of the first people to work against slavery in the United States. When he was 81, he became president of the first antislavery group in the country.

⚘ Two presidents of the United States were named after Ben. They were Franklin Pierce and Franklin D. Roosevelt.

⚘ William Franklin, one of Ben's three children, grew up to become the governor of New Jersey. Ben wanted the colonies to be free from England's rule. William wanted the colonies to stay with England. This was a problem between father and son.

GLOSSARY

colony (KOL-uh-nee)—a group of people living in a new land who still are ruled by the country from which they came. Before the Revolutionary War, the United States was 13 colonies ruled by England.

constitution (kon-stuh-TOO-shuhn)—the written ideas and laws upon which a government is based

declaration (dek-luh-RAY-shuhn)—an announcement

electricity (i-lek-TRISS-uh-tee)—a form of energy that powers lightbulbs, refrigerators, and many other things

experiment (ek-SPER-uh-ment)—a scientific way of testing or exploring an idea

independence (in-di-PEN-duhnss)—freedom from the control of other people or another government

slavery (SLAY-vur-ee)—the practice of owning other people called slaves. Slaves had to do what their owners told them to do. They were not free.

statesman (STATES-muhn)—a person who helps the government with its decisions and business

To Learn More

At the Library

Adler, David A. *A Picture Book of Benjamin Franklin.*
New York: Holiday House, 1990.

Gregson, Susan R. *Benjamin Franklin.* Mankato, Minn.:
Bridgestone Books, 2002.

Raatma, Lucia. *Benjamin Franklin.* Minneapolis:
Compass Point Books, 2001.

Scarf, Maggie. *Meet Benjamin Franklin.* New York:
Random House, 2002.

On the Web

PBS KIDS: LIBERTY'S KIDS—BENJAMIN FRANKLIN

For information about Ben, including games and facts
about the Revolution and the founding of the United States
http://pbskids.org/libertyskids/arch_who_bfranklin.html

U.S. GOVERNMENT PRINTING OFFICE: BENJAMIN FRANKLIN

For the life of the Founding Father written for kids,
with articles on his work as a printer, inventor, and
statesman, plus a timeline
http://bensguide.gpo.gov/benfranklin

FACT HOUND

Fact Hound offers a safe, fun way to find Web sites related
to this book. All of the sites on Fact Hound have been
researched by our staff.
http://www.facthound.com
1. Visit the Fact Hound home page.
2. Enter a search word related
   to this book, or type in this
   special code: 1404801863.
3. Click on the FETCH IT button.
Your trusty Fact Hound will fetch the best sites for you!

On a Trip

THE FRANKLIN INSTITUTE

222 North 20th St.
Philadelphia, PA 19103
(215) 448-1200
http://www.fi.edu
For hands-on science exhibits, the Franklin National
Memorial, several of Franklin's inventions, and models
of his study and workshop

Index